THE CATHEDRAL
Church of Christ
IN LIVERPOOL

© 2003
Published by The Bluecoat Press, Liverpool
Book design by March Design, Liverpool
Printed in China by Midas Printing International Ltd
on behalf of Compass Press Ltd

ISBN 1 904438 18 0

Contemporary photography by Barry Hale

Acknowledgments
I knew I could not bring about this story in pictures by
myself. Colin Wilkinson of The Bluecoat Press with his
photographic skills, his extensive archive of old photographs
and his publishing experience, was essential to the success
of the whole venture. Through the enthusiasm of Sam
Dawson of SPCK Liverpool Cathedral, a meeting took place
between Sam, Colin and myself at which we sketched out a
publishing plan to mark the centenary celebrations with this
new book. A plan warmly endorsed by the Right Reverend
Rupert Hoare, Dean of Liverpool. Sam, Colin and I had
given ourselves twelve months to complete the project: the
Dean wanted it in ten. We did it.

THE CATHEDRAL
Church of Christ
IN LIVERPOOL
Pictures from the first hundred years

Peter Kennerley and Colin Wilkinson
With new photography by Barry Hale

The Bluecoat Press

THE CATHEDRAL
Church of Christ
IN LIVERPOOL

Contents

FOREWORD

The Gothic splendour of Liverpool's great twentieth century Cathedral towers above the roof-tops of Georgian Rodney Street.

Words from my 7-year-old daughter about the activity of her 4-year-old sister will remain with me for ever. "Daddy, she's reading the pictures again." Having mastered the skill of reading the printed word, Rachel poured scorn on Elizabeth's ability to read pictures. Some twenty-five years later, as two highly qualified graduates, their conversation about their memories of childhood picture books reveals so much about the richness and power of the visual image.

The story of Liverpool's great twentieth century Anglican Cathedral has been told before in words in Vere Cotton's monumental *The Book of Liverpool Cathedral*, Joe Riley's *Today's Cathedral* and more recently in my *The Building of Liverpool Cathedral*. For the Cathedral's centenary celebrations I wanted to produce the pictorial story of the Cathedral, a story made possible because every stage of the progress of the building was recorded in photographs by Stewart Bale and others. I wanted to show not simply the story of the great isolated sandstone church on St James's Mount but also the story of the City of Liverpool, which took the decision to build the largest Cathedral in Britain in 1901 and which, despite the ravages of two world wars and spiralling costs, managed to complete one of the great church buildings of the twentieth century. At the start of the twentieth century, a rich, proud, confident city decided to build a Cathedral. As the walls of the Cathedral rose, the fortunes of the city declined. Today, Liverpool is once again looking confidently to the future and the completed Cathedral can celebrate its centenary knowing it has played no small part in the regeneration of one of Europe's great cities.

INTRODUCTION

1829 and 1978 John Foster's Oratory like a miniature Greek temple with Giles Gilbert Scott's masterpiece behind it. One described as "the very spirit and soul of the Greek school" and the other as "space age Gothic".

No Cathedral can be understood without some knowledge of the historical, geographical, architectural, sociological, economic, artistic, cultural, intellectual and religious environment which planned it and built it in the past and which uses it in the present. As with such Cathedrals as Durham, Lincoln, Ely and Salisbury, Liverpool Cathedral dominates the surrounding landscape to such an extent that visitors fall into the trap of thinking of it as a product of the distant past; something so massive and magnificent confuses the new visitor by giving the impression that it has been there for centuries. A very short written account of the story of the Cathedral is necessary before the visual images take over to tell a far richer story.

Visitors to such places as York, Lincoln and Chester can see ancient Cathedrals and ample evidence of significant settlements right back through the medieval period to the time of the Romans. There is no evidence to be seen above ground on the banks of the Mersey to illuminate the lives of the little settlement around a tidal inlet which formed a natural sheltered harbour. King John, aware of the potential strategic importance of that harbour, established the new town with a royal charter on 28 August 1207. A few current street names can be traced back to their thirteenth century originals as Castle Street, Dale Street and Chapel Street. The original tidal creek, or pool, offered safe anchorage, but the considerable tidal variations of the river had to be overcome. It might be said that the appointment of the engineer Thomas Steers, in 1708, marked the beginnings of what we now recognise as the townscape of Liverpool, when he drained the Pool and constructed a stone dock two hundred yards long with gates to withstand the tidal variations.

Liverpool's significance as a port grew steadily during the eighteenth century, handling large quantities of cotton, sugar and tobacco from America and the West Indies. But Liverpool cannot be proud of its increased prosperity in the eighteenth and early nineteenth century, grounded as it was upon the privateer and the slave trade. The merchant princes lived an opulent life style in the spacious new houses being built on the slopes away from the waterfront. The poor endured the degrading, grinding, insanitary existence of the courts, the cellars and the gutter.

Many of the buildings which grace the city in the twenty-first century were built in the nineteenth and Liverpool's magnificent twentieth century Cathedral was conceived in the wealth, confidence and determination of Victorian England. Though many of the great buildings of trade, commerce, the arts and government remain, Liverpool must never be allowed to forget the African slaves carried by Liverpool ships on the 'middle passage', or the hordes of starving Irish driven across the Irish Sea by the Potato Famine.

The Cathedral Church of Christ in Liverpool seen from the top of the lantern of The Metropolitan Cathedral Church of Christ the King.

The Cathedral across the roof-tops of the city from Radio City at the top of St John's Beacon.

View from the roof of Cains Brewery shows off the effectiveness of St James's Mount, the site chosen, after considerable arguments, as the ideal position for a vast Cathedral.

The Cathedral as seen from Wavertree near to the Blue Coat School.

Liverpool had been part of the vast and rich Diocese of Chester but, by the latter part of the nineteenth century, there was a determination that Liverpool should become a diocese on its own, a determination rewarded by Act of Parliament in 1880 with Bishop Ryle enthroned in the Pro-Cathedral, the old St Peter's Church in Church Street. For a variety of reasons, the first plans for a new Cathedral were thwarted and it was left to Francis James Chavasse, second Bishop, to inspire his diocese to build a great Cathedral and take the formal decision to build in the Town Hall, in June 1901.

After much argument as to the best site and a somewhat contentious open competition to find the most suitable design, Giles Gilbert Scott was appointed architect at the age of 22. Work began on the St James's Mount site and the Foundation Stone was laid by King Edward VII on Tuesday 19 July 1904.

The Bishop and the Building Committee knew that they would never live to see the completion of the enterprise: they would do what they could and hand on the continuing challenge to later generations. Queen Elizabeth II was present at the service to mark the completion of the building on 25 October 1978. Despite two world wars and spiralling inflation, the Cathedral was completed after seventy-four years of almost uninterrupted building. A Cathedral conceived in the riches of the nineteenth century, built during the economic and social turmoil of the twentieth and bequeathed to the vibrant and regenerated city of the future. For the delight and instruction of future generations, the whole building progress was recorded by the camera and this book is the visual record of the development of the largest Cathedral in Britain within the City and Diocese of Liverpool.

THE CITY PLANS A CATHEDRAL

"… The time has arrived when active steps should be taken to provide a Cathedral for the Diocese." Lord Derby

"It must in the first place be worthy of Liverpool. We must give to God not that which costs us nothing but the very best that Liverpool and the Diocese of Liverpool can afford. We must build for posterity …" Bishop Francis James Chavasse

JUNE 1901

There is no better time and place to begin this visual story of the Cathedral in the City than Monday 17 June 1901, in the Council Chamber of the Town Hall. The meeting called on that day by Bishop Francis James Chavasse encouraged those in the chamber to consider Liverpool past, present and future. People were summoned to discuss the motion, "That this public meeting of the Diocese of Liverpool is of the opinion that the time has arrived when active steps should be taken to provide a Cathedral for the Diocese."

The Town Hall itself declared the power, significance and wealth of Liverpool as a great sea port. The building, by John Wood the Younger, was completed in 1749 and gutted by fire in 1795. Reconstruction work at the hands of James Wyatt and John Foster Junior improved the building. The setting in which the proposed Cathedral was discussed spoke of civic pride and confidence.

Liverpool Town Hall, 1905.

The headline quotations in this chapter are all reported from the Town Hall meeting of 1901.

St George's Hall, 1905.

"Something to speak for God."

The Bishop told the packed Council Chamber of his experience the previous evening as he was being driven home through the city to Bishop's Palace. "There it stood out, a witness of the wealth, the wisdom, the power of the municipality of Liverpool. Why not something to speak for God in this great city as St George's Hall speaks for our great municipality?"

St George's Hall saw the combining in one building of 23-year-old Harvey Lonsdale Elmes's design for concert hall and law courts. The foundation stone was laid in 1838 to mark Queen Victoria's coronation. Elmes died before the building was complete, leaving Professor Charles Cockerell to complete the work, which was opened in 1854. In the eyes of the Bishop and the city fathers, the contrast with the Pro Cathedral must have been painful.

"Ugly and hideous."

Less than half a mile away stood the Church of St Peter's in Church Street. All that now marks the site is a brass consecration mark set into the pavement near the HMV record store. When the Diocese of Liverpool was established in 1880, St Peter's Church became the Pro-Cathedral, temporary home of the Bishop's Throne. Even the Rector of Liverpool described the church as "ugly and hideous" and the site was not suitable for a new Cathedral: "the ground on which St Peter's stands is not sufficiently large for such a Cathedral as we ought to have", and Lord Derby, who chaired the meeting, spoke of its "small size and inconvenient situation". In his introduction, His Lordship declared that the new building "will be a Cathedral worthy of the county to which it belongs."

St Peter's Church c1905. The building to the right is now Marks and Spencer on Church Street.

"The wealth, the wisdom, the power."
On the north side of William Brown Street looking across to the hall, is a handsome run of buildings which are all the products of nineteenth century Liverpool wealth and pride. The Museum was completed in 1860, the Walker Art Gallery in 1877, the Picton Library and Reading Room in 1879 and the County Sessions House in 1884. Other buildings and monuments in the vicinity include the North Western Hotel, 1871, the Wellington Column, 1863, and the Steble Fountain, 1879.

16

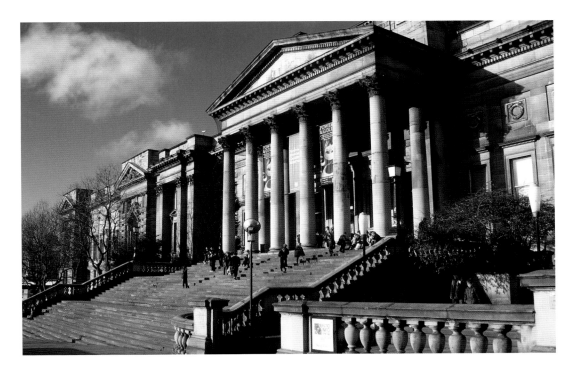

Opposite The interior of St George's Hall was described by architect Norman Shaw as "a building for all times, one of the great edifices of the world". The city which had been responsible for such secular splendour could not settle for anything second rate for its Cathedral.

1860 Liverpool Museum.

1877 Michelangelo and Raphael survey the visitors as they mount the steps of the Walker Art Gallery.

1845 The Albert Dock Warehouses: the largest group of Grade A listed buildings in the country. The massive buildings around the waters of the dock are fire-proof and built entirely of brick and iron.

"Massive monuments to maritime prosperity."

St George's Plateau and William Brown Street are the results of the wealth generated by the city but we have to move nearer to the river to find, in massive dock buildings, the source of the wealth which was later lavished on many of the prestigious civic buildings. At the time when the Cathedral was being contemplated, Liverpool docks flanked the Mersey for eight miles from Dingle to Seaforth. In 1824 Jesse Hartley was appointed Dock Engineer and some of his buildings stand as firmly today as they did when they were built. The Albert Dock Warehouses were opened by the Prince Consort in 1845 and, in the words of Quentin Hughes, "few Victorian buildings can equal their size and splendour. They stand as massive monuments to maritime prosperity in the Port of Liverpool." Many of the older warehouses built some distance from the docks were fire hazards and they offered too many opportunities for pilfering on a large scale. Hartley's buildings, in cast iron, stone and brick were right on the dockside, so that loading and unloading became more efficient. They remain the largest Grade A listed buildings in the country.

"The prosperity of business."

The twenty-first century tourist to the city, or even many of the residents, may be familiar with the famous waterfront buildings, the Cathedrals, and the St George's Hall area, but unaware of the rich architectural heritage of the nineteenth century within the commercial heart of the city from Old Hall Street to the Victoria Monument and Dale Street down to the Dock Road. The styles and materials of many of the buildings are ample evidence of "the prosperity of business" in Liverpool during the Victorian period. There is such variety, paid for by banking, insurance and business interests: Heywood's Bank Brunswick Street 1800, Queen Insurance Building Dale Street 1839, London Life Building Derby Square 1845, Branch Bank of England Castle Street 1848, Norwich Union Building Castle Street 1850, the Albany Old Hall Street 1858, Oriel Chambers Water Street 1864. It is not surprising that the Victorian Society International summer School spends time in Liverpool, a city which exhibits the whole triumph of nineteenth century architecture within a square mile.

1848 The Bank of England, architecturally one of the great buildings of the city. In the words of Quentin Hughes, "it combines a free use of Greek detail with Roman grandeur, handled with baroque versatility".

19

1840s Attractive spacious houses in Grassendale Park close to a private promenade with extensive views across the river.

1836 Gambier Terrace seen from the Cathedral across the trees in St James's Cemetery.

1824 Abercromby Square: only the residents of the houses had keys to the extensive private gardens in the centre of the Square.

1835 Stuccoed terraces in Falkner Square.

"To us who have our gardens."

From the floor of the Town Hall meeting, Edmund Rathbone from the famous Unitarian family, pointed out the spaciousness and comfort which most of the assembled group experienced at home. To walk through some of the streets and squares on the landward side of St James's Mount is to be aware of the environment in which many of the financially successful citizens lived. Regency style, well-built houses flanked wide roads and spacious, well-planted squares and gardens. Rodney Street, Falkner Street, Gambier Terrace, Abercromby Square: the owners of these properties were the people making the decisions. They were joined by the even more fortunate property owners from the residential parks and private riverside promenades: Fulwood, Grassendale and Cressington. All the architectural evidence suggests that the people of Liverpool could well afford to build a magnificent Cathedral but the Bishop was adamant in seeing the proposed Cathedral as belonging to both rich and poor, "It must be the offering of all classes" so that everyone might say, "we helped to build it."

1905 The poverty prevalent in early twentieth century Liverpool is clearly shown in this photograph of back street squalor.

The rich had their mansions in the suburbs, while the poor lived in congested, overcrowded courts, which had changed little over the previous sixty years.

"Dreary squalid streets and ... children playing in the gutter."
From the Mount downwards towards the river many people lived in very different surroundings. Living conditions in the middle of the nineteenth century were crowded even before the influx of boatloads of starving Irish immigrants; 300,000 in 1847 alone. Twenty years later, the City Engineer indicated that there were at least 18,500 insanitary houses and over 3,000 filthy, miserable, airless courts. Five thousand people were crowded into the workhouse on Brownlow Hill. No one is suggesting that the city fathers, rich merchants and senior clergy wanted to ignore the squalid living conditions of the poor, but these features must be recognised alongside the riches and splendour of the city.

An engraving looking northwards towards the familiar features of John Foster's Mortuary Chapel. In the lower right-hand corner there is evidence of work proceeding on the excavation of the catacombs.

At least as far back as the early years of the eighteenth century, the area now known as St James's Cemetery was a quarry; source of the stone of many city buildings including the Town Hall. By 1825, the good stone was exhausted and the area was laid out as a cemetery. This view is from Upper Duke Street, with Gambier Terrace on the left.

"The battle of the sites has been fought, and we don't want to hear any more about it."
The original plans for a Cathedral in the 1880s had slowly foundered for lack of public enthusiasm and support. The proposed position on the site of the old St John's Church, very close to the massive bulk of St George's Hall, had not won favour. There had been a danger that the twentieth century scheme might have run into similar difficulties. The St Peter's site, favoured by some, was too cramped and quite unsuitable. A site on Monument Place had many followers, but development there would have necessitated the demolition of a number of existing buildings and the purchase price of the site alone was very high. The Mount was ideal: it was on a sandstone ridge high above the city, docks and waterfront, and the view from the other side across the great chasm of the cemetery, was most attractive.

A view of the north end of the cemetery revealing the density of the gravestones. The Chaplain's House, seen on the left, was eventually demolished as work progressed on the Cathedral. Some of the houses on St James's Road can be seen in the background.

25

Opposite Herdman's depiction of Our Lady and St Nicholas, now Liverpool Parish Church, founded c1360 near the site of the much older St Mary del Quay. It has undergone many changes, the last after almost total destruction in the Second World War, though the tower dates from 1815. The church spire on the right is St George's Church, built on the site of Liverpool Castle and demolished in the first decade of the twentieth century.

The interior of St Peter's Church. After serving as the Pro-Cathedral until the St James's Mount site was chosen, St Peter's became surplus to requirements and, as a valuable piece of real estate in the centre of Liverpool, was sold to Woolworths as the location for their new store.

"No church building in Liverpool is nearly large enough."
In the early years of the twentieth century Liverpool was not short of churches, although a number of eighteenth century churches had been demolished: Pevsner called it a "disgraceful record". What the city did lack was a church sufficiently large to accommodate a congregation of thousands. The new Cathedral had to be vast and it had to be built to the highest standards and Chavasse reminded the gathering in the Town Hall: "It must, in the first place, be worthy of Liverpool … We must give to God not that which costs us nothing, but the very best that Liverpool and the Diocese of Liverpool can afford." The Bishop was very insistent that he was planning, not just for the city, but for the wide and varied diocese: he referred to the colliers of Wigan, the factory workers of Warrington, the glass and chemical workers of St Helens and Widnes, the engineers of Earlstown, and "the more leisured residents" of Southport. "Lastly, it must be an offering of all classes" so that even Sunday School children and poor working people would be able to say, "We helped to build it."

The earliest existing photograph of the site of the future Cathedral: it could be as early as 1901. The view is across the junction of Upper Duke Street, Rodney Street and St James's Road. The Mortuary Chapel still stands but is now completely dwarfed by the Gothic mass of the Cathedral.

At the opening of the Liverpool and Manchester Railway on 15 September 1830, the Right Hon William Huskisson MP was killed, the first victim of the railway age. He was buried at the centre of the cemetery in a round classical monument which contained a marble statue of him. The back of the long-demolished terrace of houses can be seen on the skyline.

"Not only magnificent, but almost unique among the Cathedral sites of our land."
A Parliamentary Bill received Royal Assent on 8 August 1902 authorising the Cathedral Committee to purchase St James's Mount as the site for the building of the new Cathedral.

An architectural competition had been announced in the Autumn of 1901. Of the 103 entries, six were selected to produce drawings for the second round of the competition, among them was young Giles Gilbert Scott.

"Not the best or most beautiful drawings, but the best idea and the finest conception."

The competition assessors, GF Bodley and R Norman Shaw selected the designs of the 22-year-old Giles Gilbert Scott as the finest ~ to the surprise of some, because of his young age, and the horror of others, because he was a Roman Catholic. Probably for diplomatic reasons, Scott and Bodley were appointed as joint architects, and preparations began for a great service to mark the laying of the Foundation Stone.

Above An impression of the building from Gambier Terrace. The same vantage point was used many times to produce the sequence of photographs which record the building progress.

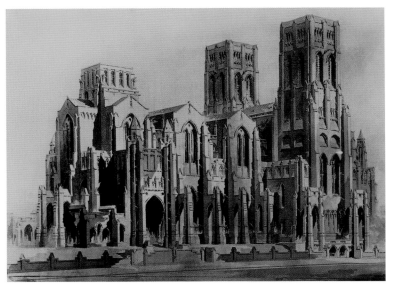

Left An artist's impression of the original 1903 design for the Cathedral. Having won the competition, Scott started again on the design and, for the rest of his life, continually made modifications to his original drawings. Even though the foundations were in place for twin towers, the committee allowed him to change his mind and accepted his plan for a massive central tower.

29

THE FIRST DECADE

"Why not something to speak for God in the midst of the great city, as St George's Hall speaks for our municipality?"

"I trust that when this Cathedral is built, it will be built not only by the thousands and tens of thousands contributed by the rich, but also by the pence of our poor, and that through the length and breadth of this great diocese, the Sunday School children and the poor working people will be able to look up to it and say, 'We helped to build it!'" Bishop Francis James Chavasse

The first decade of the century may not have made dramatic changes on the skyline of St James's Mount but those same years saw the construction of some of the most famous buildings on the Liverpool waterfront. The Pier Head began to resemble what is now famous worldwide. The Mersey Docks and Harbour Board Building was completed in 1907 and the Royal Liver Building in 1910/11. With the later Cunard Building, they were described by Pevsner as "extremely ambitious" and representing "great Edwardian imperial optimism". No one is doubting the Christian motives of Bishop Chavasse and his Cathedral team but, civic pride was as evident on St James's Mount as at Pier Head.

1908 Lord Street looking towards Church Street and the site of the Pro-Cathedral.

1907 The Mersey Docks and Harbour Board Building stands recently completed, but to our eyes it looks lonely without the Royal Liver Building and the Cunard Building.

1905 Eldon Street Flats, designed by City Engineer, James Brodie, who employed a revolutionary new building process using pre-cast concrete slabs. In striking contrast to the 'medieval' craftsmanship employed in building the Cathedral, Eldon Street epitomised the new technology of the twentieth century. Interestingly, the workers rejected the new building process and Brodie's radical ideas of replacing the slums were not developed. The flats were eventually demolished in the 1960s.

"To accommodate seven thousand if the King comes or four thousand otherwise."

The first three years of the decade were taken up with discussion, detailed planning and money-raising ~ vital behind-the-scenes activities ~ but from Tuesday 19 July 1904 onwards, progress on the site was visible and dramatic. After the agreement that King Edward VII and Queen Alexandra were to be present after lunching at the Town Hall, the site had to be made ready for the royal laying of the Foundation Stone, at 5 tons and 15 cwt, to be the heaviest stone in the whole building. A vast amphitheatre of raised wooden bench seating was prepared for an eventual congregation of 8,000. There was a choir of 1,000 voices which was to bring the ceremony to a glorious conclusion by their singing of the Hallelujah Chorus from Handel's Messiah. A cavity was prepared in the base of the stone to receive a time capsule in the form of a glass jar containing copies of that day's editions of four newspapers and various Cathedral papers. The mallet and trowel used by the King were of ivory and gold.

1904 Some final preparations for the laying of the Foundation Stone. Standing at the front are Thomas Shelmerdine, Robert Gladstone, Arthur Stanley, Frederick Radcliffe, Sir William Forwood, Bishop Chavasse, Archdeacon Madden and Mr J Alderson-Smith.

The Foundation Stone, lowered into place on 19 July 1904, remains the largest stone in the whole Cathedral. King Edward VII and Queen Alexandra can be seen on the dais to the right. Below the stone there in a cavity is a glass jar, a time capsule containing papers relating to the Cathedral project.

Good rock was of fundamental importance to the success of the whole project and the majority of the building stone was excavated from a quarry in Woolton, five miles from the Cathedral. With patient and skilled labour it was possible to bring out large blocks of stone, particularly from the lower beds. Once delivered to the Cathedral site, the huge rough blocks were sliced by the slow-cutting stone saws, at the rate of six inches an hour, before being presented to the banker masons, whose job it was, with the aid of zinc templates, to prepare every single stone by hand with the aid of a mallet and chisel.

Opposite Out of these huge boulders, a great Cathedral was built. One of the earliest photographs taken at Woolton Quarry and revealing the massive size of the sandstone blocks which were extracted. The figures of the three quarrymen give some sense of scale to the whole picture.

Left A series of photographs taken at Woolton Quarry. The bedding planes, and the systematic way in which large pieces of stone are brought out, are clearly visible.

35

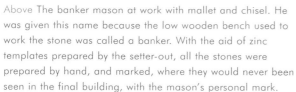

Above The banker mason at work with mallet and chisel. He was given this name because the low wooden bench used to work the stone was called a banker. With the aid of zinc templates prepared by the setter-out, all the stones were prepared by hand, and marked, where they would never been seen in the final building, with the mason's personal mark.

Top right A block of stone from the quarry on a frame saw. The steel blades, without teeth, moved backwards and forwards over the stone, lubricated by jets of water. They cut at the rate of six inches an hour.

Right View through what was to become the Chancel towards the High Altar. The rough-cut blocks from the saws are stacked in the foreground and the corrugated iron roofs of the sheds of the banker masons can be seen with finished blocks waiting to be removed to the fixer masons.

Opposite A group of banker masons at work.

1904 Early work on the Lady Chapel. In places, good load-bearing rock was near the surface, but in others, deep excavation was needed before the concrete could be poured on to the solid rock. The floor plan of the finished chapel is clearly revealed through the excavations.

1904 In the early years of the century, the blocks from the quarry were transported on wagons drawn by two horses. There were over-night stables at the quarry, and on the Cathedral site.

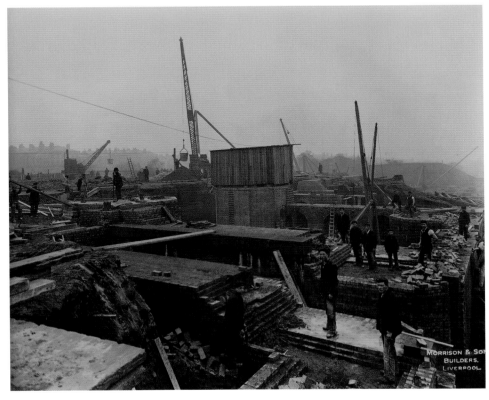

December 1905 Much of what can be seen is within the Crypt, below the level of the main floor of the Cathedral. To protect it from accident and vandals, the Foundation Stone has been clad in timber, making it resemble a garden shed. Even on the day the stone was laid, a respectably dressed man with a hammer was seen to be trying to chip off a piece of the stone.

Arches and vaulting under construction. Top left An intriguing view looking east along the south choir aisle. The Foundation Stone, encased in wood, can be seen on the right and an unexpected springer arch stone on the left. Initially, Scott did not know whether he wanted a stone choir screen. He prepared for one and, when he changed his mind, the stone was hacked off.

Top right Timber form-work being placed in preparation for the stone of the vaulting in the Lady Chapel.

Bottom left Progress as the stones of the vault are finished and placed in position.

Bottom right View of the vaulting from underneath before the final form-work has been removed.

Opposite Window tracery on the east wall of what was to become the ambulatory. The room spaces below are now part of the Cathedral Education Department.

MORRISON & SONS.
BUILDERS.
LIVERPOOL

41

November 1908 Top left A forest of rough timber scaffolding poles, lashed together with rope, from which the fixer masons had to work.

Above The procession before the consecration of the Lady Chapel on St Peter's Day, 29 June 1910. Bishop Chavasse can be seen near the centre of the picture.

Left The interior of the Lady Chapel looking towards the liturgical west. Morrison and Sons, the builders, obviously used the photograph to advertise their services.

The completed Lady Chapel with the original windows destroyed by bomb blast during the Second World War.

42.

1907 – 1910 As work went forward on St James's Mount, even more dramatic progress was to be seen at the Pier Head. The Mersey Docks and Harbour Board Building had been completed in 1907 – its dome strongly resembling that of a great church. The Cathedral was being constructed slowly, using traditional building methods, but the Royal Liver Building rose much more quickly through the use of new and experimental building techniques: it is one of the first large scale buildings using a reinforced concrete frame with a skin of granite block cladding. Pevsner wrote of the Pier Head buildings that "they represent the great Edwardian imperial optimism". The same could surely have been written of the Cathedral.

44

1910 ~ 1920

"In an age of materialism, uncertainty and doubt, the great Cathedral rising on St James' Mount is a witness to the fact that there are still men and women amongst us who have convictions, to whom God and Christ and Eternity are real, and who are animated by a faith which is able alike to sustain a nation in the agony of an appalling war, and could lead its citizens to consecrate part of their wealth to glorify God, by the erection of the most noble House that they could devise for His worship and honour." Bishop Francis James Chavasse

1911 The building of the Cathedral continued during a period of increased public agitation, illustrated here with crowds gathered on St George's Plateau in support of the widespread transport strike.

So threatening was the prospect of a prolonged strike, that the government ordered troops to be deployed in the city. Police despatched from other cities used primitive armoured wagons to transport them through the troubled city.

48

"Mr Gilbert Scott submitted a proposal and drawings to alter the original design ..."

The General Committee met briefly in the Town Hall after the service on St Peter's Day 1910 to mark the Consecration of the Lady Chapel, only six years to the day after the laying of the Foundation Stone. It was forecast that the chancel and eastern transept would be completed in a little over four years, at an estimated cost of £140,000. How wrong they were, as the new decade heralded a period of unprecedented upheaval and change.

Scott's proposal to radically change his original design by replacing the twin towers over the Transept with one massive central tower was but a part of more fundamental change. The nave was shortened, but the crossings between eastern and western Transepts and a huge central space, would provide unobstructed views of the east end. Scott was delighted, "It has always astonished me that the Committee allowed a young man in his twenties completely to alter a design chosen in a competition by two eminent assessors." Realistic estimates suggested that the new portion of the Cathedral would be ready for use by 1917.

A series of excellent photographs charts the progress of the building, but the archive photographs cannot reflect the turmoil and carnage which followed on from the outbreak of the Great War on 4 August 1914. There was a shortage of skilled labour, a slowing of the inflow of new money and steep rises in cost. "It is a measure of the appalling casualties in the first World War, that during the four and a quarter years that it lasted, more than a third of the members of the Executive Committee had suffered bereavement; nine had lost sons, one a grandson, and one a son-in-law, all killed in action."

As a vitally important seaport for transatlantic traffic, the city enjoyed reasonable prosperity during the war years but poverty quickly returned. Triggered by a police strike, August Bank Holiday 1919 saw the worst riots in the city since the eighteenth century. There were soldiers in St George's Hall and tanks were drawn up on the plateau.

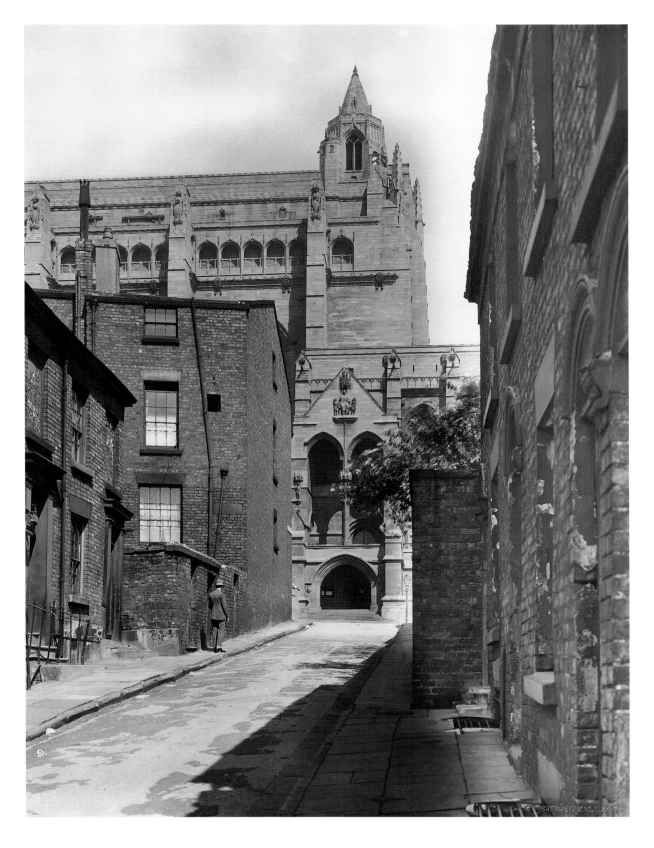

c1918 Opposite The east end of the Cathedral. The Lady Chapel is on the left and the octagonal Chapter House, with its conical roof, is on the right. The east window has not yet been installed. Much of the building is still covered in timber scaffolding lashed together with rope, rope which tended to shrink when soaked by rain and then slacken when it dried.

Left The view up Nile Street to the Children's Porch of the Lady Chapel.

1921 King Edward VII had been present to lay the Cathedral Foundation stone in 1904. William Gascombe John's statue is well placed at the Pier Head. By the 1920s the unfinished Cathedral was becoming as important a feature on the city skyline as the waterfront buildings.

1913 The classical facade to the Faculty of Arts Building at the University. The University, like the Cathedral, was an important symbol of Liverpool's civic importance.

1916 The Cunard Building, headquarters of the Cunard Steamship Company. The strength and dignity of the building reflects the importance of the Port of Liverpool, particularly for transatlantic shipping. Captain Smith, of the Titanic, which sank in 1912, is commemorated in a small window in the Cathedral.

1913 The Adelphi Hotel – it might have been called Cunard splendour on shore. Frank Atkinson, the architect, was also responsible for the design of luxurious interiors for passenger liners.

THE TWENTIES

"It was evident that to mark such an occasion no repetition of a traditional form would suffice; that it would not be enough to collect together a variety of ancient ceremonies and formulae and to combine them into an Office. What was needed was a service which, while fulfilling all that past experience could suggest, should possess a coherence, a rhythm, an appropriateness of its own for the circumstances of today. Such a service must be the work, not of a liturgies expert (if this means a student of past precedents), but of a creative artist who perceived what the ceremony signified, knew how to interpret its significance in apposite technique, and could enable the congregation to experience and share in the dramatic movement of the whole." Charles Raven

Without the slightest doubt, the greatest Cathedral achievement of the 1920s rested, not in the brick, stone and glass of the building, but in the great Service of Consecration on 19 July 1924. Until that date, no English Cathedral had been consecrated on an entirely new site since Salisbury in 1225.

With his typical modesty, Francis James Chavasse, the inspiration behind the whole project, resigned his bishopric in 1923, so that a new and younger man could preside at the Consecration in the following year. He was succeeded by Albert Augustus David ~ liberal, imaginative, innovative, highly intelligent and with the honesty to admit that he did not have the liturgical skills to devise the special service which was required. That work fell to the Rev Frederick William Dwelly, Vicar of Emmanuel Church in Southport. There are stories of Dwelly in flannels and cricket shirt, running round the building during rehearsals organising the processions. King George V and Queen Mary were to be present and inexplicably arrived at the Cathedral 15 minutes ahead of schedule and were prevailed upon to wait quietly in a doorway and watch the entry of the final processions. The service was the first evidence in the Cathedral of the genius of the man who was later to become the first Dean of Liverpool. As the *Church Times* reported, "If any person at all is entitled to take credit for the events of this week in Liverpool Cathedral, that person, above all, is Mr Dwelly".

One year after Consecration, the first soil on the new portion of the site was turned. Worship pervaded the completed chancel and transept as construction got under way on the most dramatic portion of the whole building ~ the central space and the tower. In the autumn of 1925, 300 tons of spoil were coming off the site every working day ~ 12,000 tons in all between August and December. Fourteen thousand feet of foot-square timbers were required during the laying of the foundations.

Opposite Though the proud city and diocese celebrated the Consecration of the new Cathedral, too many of the population were still living in the most cramped and squalid conditions, as revealed by hundreds of photographs which were taken by the City Engineer's Department. The courts were slowly demolished, although the last survived until the 1960s.

1925 Left Heavy traffic lines the Landing Stage. Before the Mersey Tunnel was constructed, the only way to cross the river was by ferry.

1920 Below A degrading experience as dockers queue for work outside Stanley Dock. The mass unemployment in the inter-war period was deeply felt across the whole country.

SALTNEY ST. MAR 8 1920

1924 Even in its incomplete state, the Cathedral dominates the urban landscape. This view from the top of one of the Pier Head buildings shows the upper storeys of the brick and stone striped White Star building and the classical grandeur of the old Custom House, a later victim of wartime bombing.

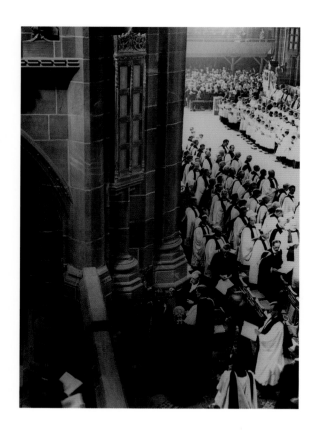

Above The Bishop uses a template to mark the place of one of the Consecration Crosses, the carving of which actually took place during the course of the service. The wooden gallery in front of the temporary brick wall which was used to increase the seating capacity, can be seen in the top right-hand corner. The gallery proved popular and was not demolished until just before the central space came into use.

Top right Twenty years to the day from the laying of the Foundation Stone, the incomplete Cathedral was consecrated – only the Chancel and eastern Transepts were finished. Frederick William Dwelly, later to be the first Dean, leads the procession towards the door in the temporary brick wall which separated the finished work from the building site. Bishop Albert Augustus David, third Bishop of Liverpool, is seen carrying his Bishop's crosier.

Right The signing of the Consecration Document. Queen Mary leans forward to sign and King George V stands on her left. The Chancel is filled to capacity with clergy and choir.

Post 1926 View across the Chancel arch from the Derby Transept. Even though there was another two thirds of the building to be completed, the vast spaces of the Cathedral were most impressive, particularly during great services accompanied by one of the largest and most comprehensive pipe organs to be found anywhere in the world.

18.

1926 View from the roof of the North East Transept looking down on to the next stage of building from which the central space and the tower would eventually rise.

Behind the brick wall at the top of the picture the worshipping life of the Cathedral proceeded to establish itself, while banker and fixer masons are at work on the new portion.

The base of the pier to support the north west tower arch. The area in the foreground is now part of the Welsford Porch, home of the Cathedral Refectory. The fixer masons worked ahead of the bricklayers, as can be seen from the lower stages of the pier.

1928 Part of the site seen from the north side as the walls of the central space and the South West Transept rise. The two figures on the top of the wall below the jib of the crane, are almost certainly Sir Giles Scott and Owen Pittaway, Clerk of Works.

1928 Opposite View across the central space into what was to become the North West Transept, present home of the SPCK shop. The legs of the crane soar skywards.

1922 Right Another Scott building in Liverpool: St Paul's Church, Derby Lane. The high transepts are reminiscent of earlier designs for the Cathedral. The strength of the central tower and the confidence in the use of plain surfaces are Scott features. It is easy to forget the varied extent of Scott's work from the red telephone box to Cambridge University Library and Battersea Power Station.

1930 Right bottom The Cenotaph on the plateau in front of St George's Hall. The dignified figures in the bronze panels are by Herbert Tyson Smith, the man who carved the inscription on the Foundation Stone of the Cathedral in 1904, and brother-in-law of Edward Carter Preston whose work is much in evidence in the Cathedral. His daughter, Julia, is a celebrated Liverpool potter.

1932 Opposite Herbert J Rowse's Martins Bank Building exhibits the same confidence that was the foundation of so many of Liverpool's impressive Victorian and Edwardian buildings, a 'cathedral' to commerce.

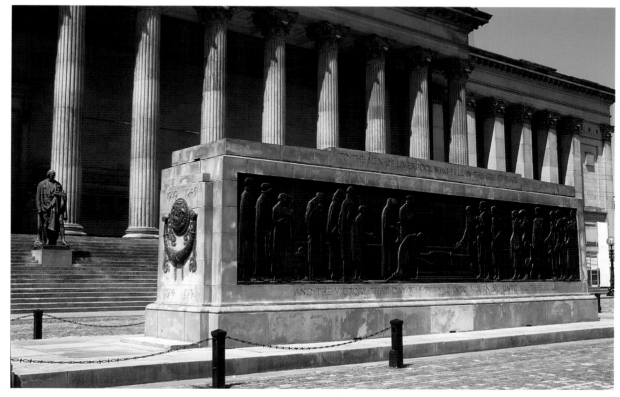

66

THE THIRTIES

"A Liverpool Cathedral should be readily seen from many parts of the city, and, above all, by the life of the city, the river, with its ships and docks. All Cathedrals should be specially conspicuous by tower or spire, and these again should be made more conspicuous by some great figure of white or gold, the guardian of the city; and some further glory of windvanes, telling the windshifts, and great bells telling the hours and their quarters, and ringing for the city's joys; in this city, for the ship launched, or the ship come home …

This Cathedral of Liverpool, the greatest of modern Cathedrals, is a Church of the Resurrection. It comes into the life of our time, in a decade when all the ways of life known to us from childhood have to be remade, when the nation has to be recreated, with what difficulty we do not yet know, but no doubt with much." John Masefield

The two paragraphs quoted from John Masefield's address to the Cathedral company in 1931 are particularly significant when seen together. Liverpool Cathedral's most massive feature, the great central tower, was largely the product of the 1930s. The implications of Masefield's second paragraph are even more pertinent than he may have realised at the time. There is nothing in the vistas of the central space or the 331 feet one and a half inches of the tower even to hint at any of the social, economic and political problems of the decade. There seems nothing in the structure which in any sense reflects the Wall Street crash of 1929 and the ensuing economic depression, or the world's inevitable descent into World War Two.

Work on the central space began before the Vestey family's offer to finance the building of the tower. Vere Cotton informed the readers of *The Bulletin* of the immense resources handled between 1925 and 1935: Two million cubic feet of rock had been quarried at Woolton; 4,700 lorry loads of stone weighing 26,000 tons had been delivered to the site and set as finished stone 310,000 cubic feet in volume and 21,000 tons in weight. 4,750,000 bricks had been laid. Placed end to end they would have stretched 675 miles, or stacked on top of each other, made a column 40 times the height of Everest. Not surprisingly, some of the most dramatic photographs of the whole building programme were taken during the decade.

The formal establishment of the Dean and Chapter did not take place until 1931 when Frederick William Dwelly was installed as the first Dean: a post he was to hold until his retirement in frail physical and mental health in 1955. Even before the completion of the central space and the Nave, Liverpool Cathedral became world famous for the imaginative and splendid character of its services, devised by the liturgical genius of its first Dean. Unencumbered by medieval statutes, the twentieth century Cathedral became the centre of an important ministry in the city and region. In Charles Raven's words: "The great communal services, medical, educational and artistic, financial, industrial and commercial, were in fact ministries and vocations; and that the first task of the Church was to arouse the consciousness of God, to foster worship and the practice of His Presence, and to show how this experience could be related to and must transform the whole conduct of our daily life."

1931 saw the establishment of the Dean and Chapter but the fall of the Labour Government and the establishment of a National Government under Ramsay MacDonald with the task of shoring up a collapsing economy with unemployment numbers rising above two million. Expenditure on the building was not diminished, as is reflected in the rising numbers at work on the site from 137 in 1928 to 187 in 1932. That same year brought news of architect Edward Maufe's winning design for a new Cathedral for Guildford. Across the Atlantic, the Empire State Building, the tallest building in the world, had been opened in 1931.

The Cathedral community was not unaware of the wider national and international events of the decade; the death of King George V, abdication of Edward VIII and accession of George VI, the Spanish Civil War, and the spread of German power. The service paper for Sunday 3 September 1939 read, "Because of the evacuation of the children of the choir, the daily services in the Cathedral will be non-choral. The Congregation is asked to sing with full heart and voice all the music of the Sunday services."

September 1934 This dramatic photograph was taken from the top of Lewis's department store in Renshaw Street. St Luke's Church stands prominently at the bottom of Leece Street.

1933 The Foundation Stone was laid for Sir Edward Lutyens's design for the Metropolitan Roman Catholic Cathedral. The wooden model is impressive and the finished building would have been the second largest church in Christendom after St Peter's in Rome. Work started on the Crypt but ceased in 1941 and was never restarted. The post-war world could not face the meteoric rise in costs and other less expensive solutions were sought. Eventually Frederick Gibberd's design was accepted because it could be built for a million pounds.

An artist's impression of the Cathedral buildings standing at either end of Hope Street. In the words of Doreen Yarwood in *The Architecture of England*, "If it had been built it would have been the greatest monument to modern Neo-Classicism in Britain, in much the same way as Scott's Liverpool Cathedral, near by, is the last great monument to Neo-Gothic architecture."

1930 Opposite From the temporary brick wall through the canyon-like area soon to become the central space. Once again, the simple sheds to protect the banker masons from the worst of the weather have been moved, so that the stones could be finished as close as possible to the walls into which they were to be inserted.

Early 1930s The incomplete circular tracery was to form the rose window to contain the picture of Moses with the tablets of the law on the north side of the central space. The sturdy timber planking platform from which the masons worked can be seen in the foreground.

Early 1930s Three workmen stand looking down through what was to become a great rose window. The massive timbers in the foreground are there to support the platform from which the masons worked during the construction of the under-tower vaulting.

1934 The timber centreing for the under-tower vault is here being assembled. The shape of arches and vaulting was first constructed in wood. When the stone and brick had been laid systematically on the wooden frames, they were removed.

1936 The under-tower vault nearing completion. The circular bell trap, just large enough to accommodate the largest bell, can be seen at the top of the vault.

1932 Work on the final stages of the vaulting in the South West Transept.

1935 A dramatic shot of part of the steel frame devised by structural engineer, Burnard Geen, to support nearly 35 tons of bells. All the weight from the centre of the belfry floor is carried downwards and outwards by the frame and on to a reinforced concrete girdle which is enclosed within the tower walls.

Where was the photographer? An ingenious shot almost certainly taken by an intrepid photographer suspended in the bucket of the crane. It gives a vivid impression of the high-level platform from which the builders operated when working high in the tower.

1935 Opposite The classic view across the cemetery. The very top of the inverted nest of steel girders to support the weight of the bells can be seen below the cranes.

1937 A beautiful juxtaposition of Classical and Gothic as the steps, pillars and lintel of the Mortuary Chapel frame the partly built tower and the massive Nave arch.

c1938 One of the most attractive and romantic views of the Cathedral from down in the cemetery. The graves are beginning to show some signs of neglect but as yet no signs of vandalism. The tower is still encased in tons of timber scaffolding, a feature which was to cause great concern at the outbreak of war because of the damage which might be caused even by even a single incendiary bomb.

Fixer masons and bricklayers at work over 200 feet up on the walls of the tower. Note the complete lack of safety measures – the cloth cap had not yet been replaced by the hard-hat. The architect had the greatest admiration for the skills of his masons as they coped with the overall battering on the tower and the gradually narrowing of the walls themselves.

1937 Excavations beneath the central space, an area now housing the chair store and the maintenance department. The temporary brick wall can be seen in the background. The Carter Preston figures on the porch doorways are encased in timber for their protection.

84

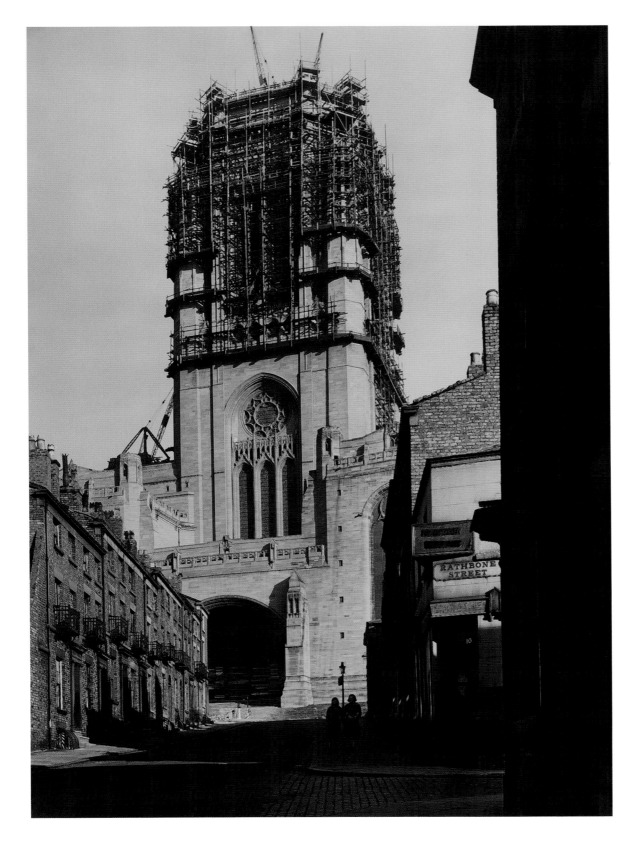

c1939 The classic view of the Cathedral from Washington Street. The photographic archive contains a sequence of different versions of this view as the stonework is finished, the timber removed, and the oak louvres fitted. It was this view that was most missed by the people of Liverpool when the area in front of the Cathedral was redeveloped in the 1980s.

THE FORTIES

"For the second time during the building of the Cathedral, England finds itself engaged in a struggle of such magnitude as to demand the concentration of all its resources of man power and material if victory is to be achieved ...

The policy of the Committee can be stated quite shortly ~ it is to go steadily ahead as far as human and material resources permit, but of course, no attempt will be made to claim that work on the Cathedral is in any sense a reserved occupation and any hope of completing the work by next summer, must, in the changed circumstances, be finally abandoned. In any case, a great Inaugural Service, or rather series of services, such as had been planned, would be unthinkable in time of war and whatever progress is achieved with the actual building must be postponed until peace is once more restored to a troubled world." Vere Cotton

For the Cathedral and City of Liverpool it is probably true to say that the Forties began the day the Second World War was declared in September 1939. Though this war would see nothing to compare with Ypres, Passchendaele, Gallipoli and the Somme, the physical damage to the city in the bombing was devastating. The line of docks from Dingle to Seaforth was of enormous strategic and economic importance. That the damage to the Cathedral from bombs was not greater is remarkable. Many windows were lost and much damage sustained in areas outside

occupied by the builders, and yet the single direct hit by a bomb caused remarkably little damage.

King George VI and Queen Elizabeth visited the city and the Cathedral in November 1940 and the King's reported comment became a rallying call to the community: "Keep going, whatever you do, even if you can only go on in a small way." The builders had to keep going, even though with a drastically reduced work force because, in 1939, the tower walls had risen to 279 feet above floor level and the whole structure was clad in highly flammable timber scaffolding. The May Blitz of

1941 was the worst week in the city's history when night after night there was heavy bombing and 1,453 people were killed. Five hundred bombers flew over the city during one night alone.

Solemn Entrance in Time of War in July 1941 brought the almost completed central space into use, but it was not until the following year that the final finial was complete at the top of the tower and the capping-out ceremony could take place ~ even though the tower had no roof because of cement restrictions. In an unexpected way, the local inhabitants were aided by the Cathedral in that the

authorities invited them to use two robing rooms, now known as the Western Rooms, as night-time air raid shelters.

Though Germany and Japan were defeated, post-war social and economic conditions worsened. Food rationing increased in severity after the end of the war, with even loaves of bread rationed. Fuel supplies were dangerously low. Housing shortages were intense. 1947 was one of the most severe winters for years. To start up the building progress again amidst the post-war exhaustion and austerity must have been very difficult. It was over 40 years since the prosperous, confident, empire-building attitudes of 1904 had laid the foundation stone of the largest Anglican church in the world. Miraculously, that building had escaped serious war damage, but shortage of materials, money and manpower must have cast an impenetrable gloom over the whole Cathedral world. The Archbishop of York's words in 1945 were calculated to help restore confidence and raise flagging spirits: "At this, your annual service, there must be in all your hearts profound thanksgiving that this great Cathedral has suffered so little damage during the destruction caused by the European war. It has not indeed escaped unharmed, for it has shared in the injuries inflicted on your city, but within and without it has received no irreparable damage. And although, during the war, work on a large scale has inevitably to be suspended, a small devoted band of workers has continued uninterruptedly in perfecting what has been commenced, in repairing what has been damaged, and in making ready for the day when once again it will be possible to go forward with the completion of this splendid building."

c1941 Bomb-battered Liverpool with the Cathedral as such a prominent target so near to the river and the docks. Because of the danger to the timber scaffolding from the nightly aerial bombardments in 1940 and 1941, many members of the Cathedral community, including Dean Frederick Dwelly, lived in the Cathedral on fire-watching duties.

November 1940 King George V and Queen Elizabeth visited the damaged city so that they could identify themselves with the people during the dangerous days of war. The King's words to the Dean were an important note of encouragement, "Keep going, whatever you do, even if you can only go on in a small way."

As the scaffolding is removed, the fine detail of the stone becomes clear for the first time.

c1942 The parapet at the top of the tower walls, over 300 feet above the floor of the Cathedral. Though the walls were slowly reaching completion, the roof was not, because no license was available to enable sufficient cement to be acquired for the concrete beams and roof.

1942 On 20 February, the final pinnacle on the tower was completed to a height of 331 feet one and a half inches. Note the flimsy wooden platform. What the camera did not show was that there was no roof on the tower and the sheer drop down to the floor of the belfry. It was a very cold day and the architect complained that, when asked to remove his hat, he almost turned blue.

Above One pinnacle was struck by lightning and badly damaged before a lightning conductor could be fixed. Even now, when the building is fully protected, it is alarming when the building is struck.

Left A signed photograph of the architect to "my friend Dwelly". Although his offices in London suffered badly during the Blitz, Sir Giles stayed at work on his Cathedral and produced plans, never used because of rising costs, for the west wall.

THE FIFTIES

"In Liverpool Cathedral we have a vast building in a modern city erected for no commercial, industrial or economic purpose; a large portion of its cost has been defrayed by hard-headed businessmen. The building work has been carried on continuously for nearly 50 years, including two devastating world wars; even the Blitz of the last war failed to put a stop to the work for, with the aid of a few elderly workmen, stone upon stone continued to be laid on the Central Tower, and in defiance of the bombs, this building continued to go up while buildings all around were crashing to the ground. So was displayed the magnificence of the human spirit that no materialism can quench."

When Princess Elizabeth formally opened the Rankin Porch, it was 45 years since her Great Grandfather laid the foundation stone. Unfortunately, at the end of 1949, there were only 37 men at work on the site and this included 11 masons and only one apprentice. Progress was slow but Vere Cotton reported that 1950 saw more progress than any year since the war and the end of the year saw an increased work force of 76, with 19 masons and 4 apprentices.

1951 saw a very public proclamation that the Cathedral scheme was making progress. On 19 November, the bells rang out for the first time across the roof-tops of the city and earlier in the year, on 17 June, the Cathedral had celebrated its Jubilee, the fiftieth anniversary of the Town Hall meeting and the decision to embark on the project. The whole world had changed beyond recognition. Slow progress was made on the building, hampered by lack of finance and skilled manpower but the changes in the world, the nation and the city, were immense: a coronation, Everest climbed, the four-minute mile, DNA, nuclear weapons, Elvis Presley, Rock 'n' Roll, two of the Beatles were at school just over the road from the Cathedral, *The Archers* and *The Goon Show*, the Mini.

The fifties saw the retirements or deaths of a number of people who had given a lifetime of service to the Cathedral: Sir Frederick Radcliffe, Dean Dwelly, Harry Goss Custard, Owen Pittaway but the work continued with new leaders. The tower was roofed, the bells installed, the Western Rooms completed and decorated and, rather slowly, the walls of the first bay of the nave began to rise, but by 1954, shortage of funds led to a cutting of the skilled work force. The following year a successful appeal was launched to raise £500,000.

Right top One thousand four hundred and fifty-three people were killed during a single week during the May Blitz of 1941, but painfully slowly in the late forties and early fifties life returned and slow progress could be made on the still-unstarted Cathedral nave. Poverty still blighted the city and post-war austerity compounded the difficulties felt in many deprived communities across Liverpool.

Right A short-lived bonus for local children. As the site in front of the Cathedral was cleared, it found a temporary use as a playground.

Opposite top left Liners returned to Pier Head after their War-time absence. Right Crowds enjoying the sun at New Brighton.

Opposite bottom left Workers at Meccano with their novel production line. Right Improved social provision included new wash-houses, which were important communal meeting places.

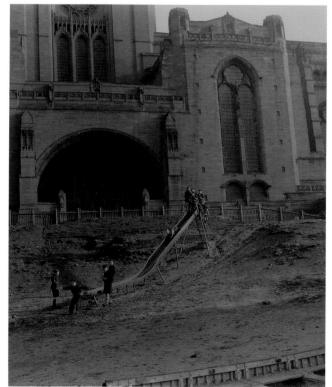

1950 The view up Washington Street as work commences on the installation of the oak louvres in the bell chamber.

The devastating bomb damage took years to remedy. Little had been left on one side of Church Street and Lord Street was flattened. However, eventually life started to return to normal and slowly, at the Cathedral, new work began on the first bay of the Nave and the Dulverton Bridge.

1940 In the 1912 bequest of Thomas Bartlett, there was a sum of money to provide a peal of bells for the Cathedral, bells which could not be accommodated until the tower was complete. Twelve of the bells are shown in this photograph shortly after their delivery from the Whitechapel Foundry, the oldest in the world.

1951 The bourdon bell, Great George, was cast by the John Taylor Foundry in Loughborough and delivered to the Cathedral early in the summer of 1951. Its journey on a low-loader lorry must have caused interest along the route

The diameter of the bell is nine feet six inches and the bell trap only six inches more. The first attempt to hoist it failed because the bell had started to rotate and twisted the cables. The peal is the highest and heaviest anywhere in the world.

7 May 1951 A team of twelve men assembled on the floor of the bell chamber around a two-handled winch. The group was divided into three teams of four to be changed every ten minutes. They winched at the rate of four inches a minute and the lift took ten hours.

THE SIXTIES
AND SEVENTIES

"During five reigns this Committee has laboured unceasingly to finance, plan, and build the greatest English Cathedral since Wren rebuilt St Paul's after the Fire of London.

Looking back, it would be difficult to find any period in history more unpropitious for the executing of a project of this magnitude.

For ten of the fifty-seven years during which the Cathedral has been building, the two greatest wars in history deflected the thoughts, the wealth and the man-power of the nation to other more pressing needs. The great economic slump following the First War, and the inflationary consequences of the Second, raised problems no less complex than the war years themselves, yet in spite of this well-nigh overwhelming series of difficulties, the Liverpool Cathedral Committee has never for an instant faltered in its task, and the ever increasing costs of building have been met by the increasing generosity of the city and the diocese." *Sir Alan Tod*

The words of Sir Alan Tod were delivered in April 1961 at the service to mark the dedication of the first bay of the Nave. He went on to inform the congregation that every stone in 1961 cost twelve times as much as it had done in 1904. Only the two final bays of the Nave and the west front were left for completion. In a changed world, the final 17 years were going to be difficult. Scott had produced plans for the west front in 1942, but by the early sixties, that wall alone would have cost £1,300,000. Wisely, a new and cheaper plan was adopted, but even so, in 1967, it was projected that the three bays of the Nave and west front would cost more than had been spent on the whole of the rest of the building.

The Dean by that time was Edward Patey, an imaginative, articulate priest who faced with honesty the enormity of the task of completing the building and was concerned as to whether or not this was the best use of money in the 1960s. In the 1967 appeal in the Town Hall he said, "But a Dean is neither the director of a building operation, nor the curator of an ecclesiastical museum, nor the promoter of a tourist attraction. He is the servant of the Church of God. My job (in collaboration with my colleagues) is to use the Cathedral as an instrument for the Kingdom of God. This is our yardstick."

There were huge problems to be faced: the building company went into liquidation, the city planned to build a raised motorway parallel with the Rankin Porch, and inflation was rocketing. Though Liverpool might be seen as the centre of the swinging sixties and home-ground of the Beatles, everything had changed from the proud, rich and confident Edwardian Liverpool of 1901.

Though much tidying up was left to be done, the completion of the Cathedral Church of Christ in Liverpool was marked by a service in the presence of Her Majesty Queen Elizabeth II on 25 October 1978.

Above The Cathedral in the early 1970s, shortly before the housing on the west side was demolished.

1965 Progress on the second bay of the Nave. The general decay of the houses on the slope in front of the Cathedral is evident. Visitors were beginning to approach the Cathedral through a tangle of urban dereliction. The proud, rich and successful city that had embarked on the building of a great Cathedral had changed and the economic pressures were enormous. Questions were being asked as to whether or not the project should be brought to a close with a temporary concrete wall. Dean Edward Patey was determined that the building should be finished and said in 1968, "Architectural fashions may come and go. But I believe that in every century men and women of taste and sensitivity will look at our building high above the Mersey and say, 'This really is a Cathedral!'"

December 1975 The erection of the timber form-work for the west end arch. Notice that timber scaffolding poles have given way to metal.

Carl Edwards, stained glass artist, at work in his studio. Scott had talked to Edwards as they wandered round the building and the windows in the Nave were to be the finest in the Cathedral. "What he wanted was that light from the windows should be controlled, especially at the east and west end; these windows to be full of colour and restrict light, but all windows north and south should emit as much light as possible. Great passages of light streaming across the main body of the Cathedral would illuminate the stonework, vaulting and arches, adding drama to the structure; a grandeur in space and form which one finds in the work of Piranesi."

106

Brothers Tom and John Rowbottom, life-long Cathedral stone masons. John worked on the building for 49 years. His funeral was held at the Cathedral and his ashes were interred in Founders' Plot.

Carver Tom Murphy at work on the royal coat of arms to go above the interior of the west doors. The clay model from which he worked can be seen in the background.

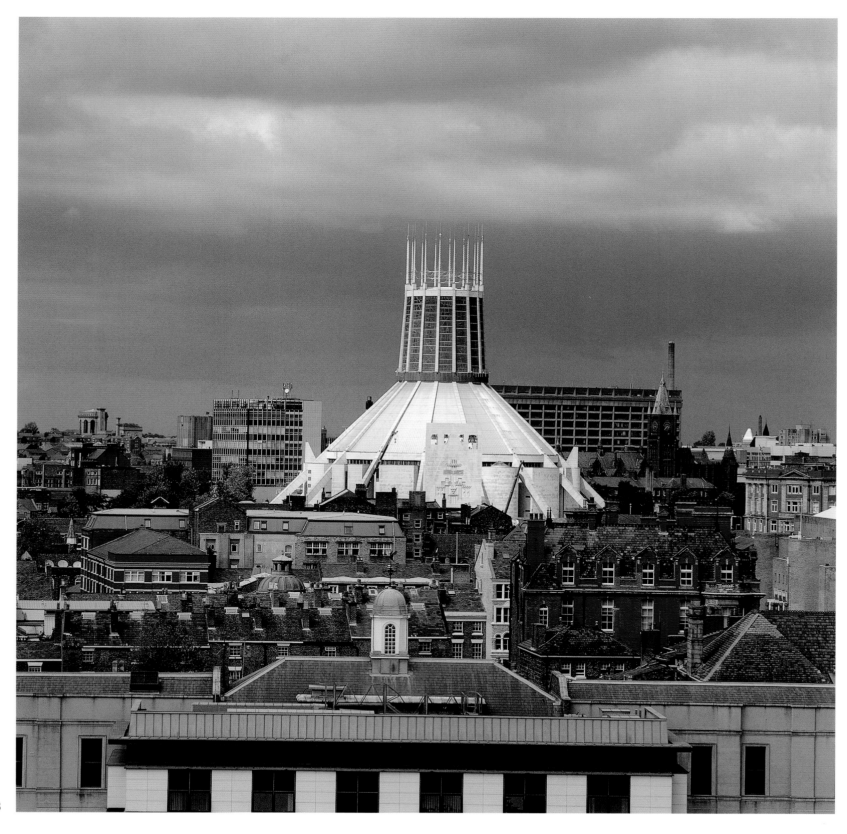

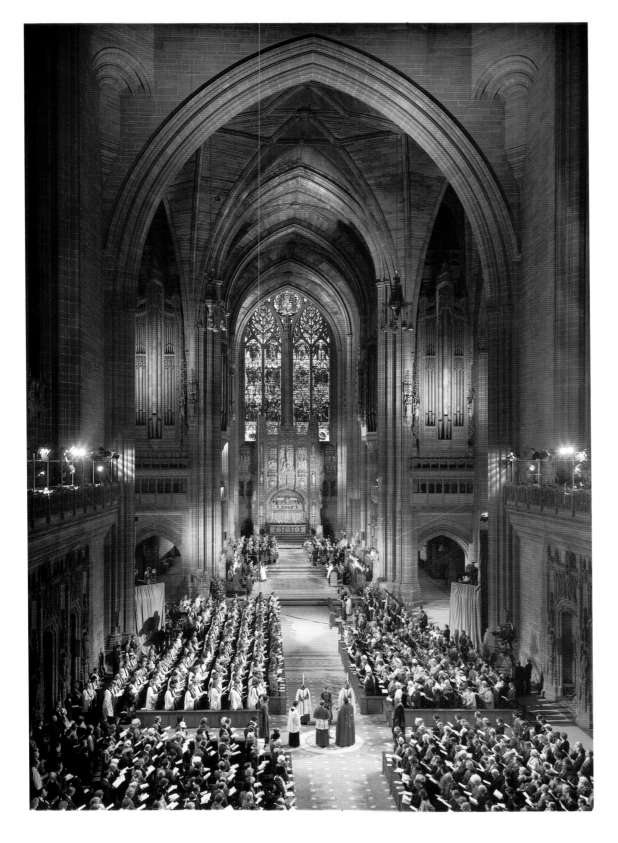

Although started many years after the Anglican Cathedral, the Metropolitan Cathedral was completed in 1967 to the design of Sir Frederick Gibberd and is, in the words of Quentin Hughes, "undoubtedly the major modern architectural attraction of the city".

25 October 1978 Seventy-four years after the laying of the Foundation Stone, Queen Elizabeth II attended the great service to mark the completion of the Cathedral Church of Christ in Liverpool.

109

May 1982 Pope John Paul II, Head of the Roman Catholic Church on his historic visit to Liverpool and both of its Cathedrals. When the Cathedral was first planned it was inconceivable that a Pope would ever be an honoured guest in the Anglican Cathedral.

THE EIGHTIES
AND NINETIES

"At last we've got a Dean who understands finance."
Member of the Cathedral Congregation

*"While our primary role is to let the Cathedral help people in
their encounter with God, you can't ignore the context in
which we're working. It is desperately important that we
create new jobs in the city because that's what gives people a
sense of pride and meaning." Edward Patey*

*"Your building is magnificent, but why can't the city give it
an appropriate setting?" Tourist*

*"A major site surrounds the magnificent Anglican Cathedral.
It is a city site of world importance. I have discussed with the
City and the County Councils, who own the site, the way in
which it may be developed, in keeping with its location."
Michael Heseltine*

*"Wealth creation and job creation are an essential part of the
Church's ministry. Having invested so much time and money
in the building of a great Cathedral, we must now be involved
in the rehabilitation of the surrounding city." Derrick Walters*

In 1894, Canon Ken Riley preached a powerful sermon at the annual Civic Service during a period of painful social and economic difficulty in the city.

"Exactly ten years ago, passing the Cathedral late one Sunday evening, I came across a man crawling up the steps on his hands and knees. Going up to him I saw that his wrists were cut and there was blood all over the steps. The ambulance came within three minutes and he was whisked off into the night, blue light flashing and bell clanging. I don't know the end of his story: I don't know whether we got to him in time or not. Some would say he was a representative of Liverpool: hurt, desperate, hopeless ~ and they would stop there.

Yet he was on the steps of Liverpool Cathedral ~ built by the people of Liverpool in our time; begun in 1904 and enshrining the hopes and aspirations of Liverpool through bad times as well as good; through the thirties Depression and two World Wars. Perhaps the total scene that night more truly represents our city. Yes, there are those who are hurting and hurting badly ~ as there are in every other city ~ what the poet HD Carberry calls "hurt creatures, sobbing out their sorrow to the rhythm of the blues". Yet that is not the whole story. There is also what he calls a "magnificent reaching out, a yearning for something that is beyond all that is sham and shoddy, part of that divine discontent with things as they are, a reaching out for things as they might be, even things which seem beyond ourselves, of which this building is a sign."

The Canon went on to speak of turning dreams into reality ~ one of those dreams being the renewal of Liverpool. But the decade had begun disastrously with the Toxteth Riots in the summer of 1981: political, social and economic unrest bursting out in successive nights of violence less than half a mile from the Cathedral. With Michael Heseltine appointed as the new Minister for Merseyside, the urban dereliction on the Cathedral site became a matter for urgent action. A new Dean, Derrick Walters, was installed in 1983: a graduate of the London School of Economics and the right person to fight for urban regeneration on the Cathedral site at a time when the city was in the political grip of the Militant Tendency. The success of the total building scheme would have faltered but for the initiatives taken by Dean and Chapter when confidence in the city was so low.

Michael Heseltine was wholly supportive of the plans for the total development of the Cathedral site: "I share wholeheartedly your reaction to the history of neglect of this site and your hopes for the future." By 1986, the houses of Cathedral Close were opened formally by Sir Douglas Lovelock, First Church Estates Commissioner. There was so little confidence in the city at that time that some people feared there would be no buyers for the houses being built in another two courts, so the Chapter took responsibility for leading the whole project and leased the houses to Liverpool Polytechnic for student accommodation.

The success of the Cathedral site project led to an even more extensive site. Less than half a mile from the Cathedral were 40 acres of urban dereliction and decay. Project Rosemary, as the scheme was called, needed investment of £54 million and, as the photographs reveal, was a complete success. At the beginning of the twentieth century, a rich and confident city had set out to build a Cathedral. By the end of that century, that same Cathedral was highly influential in helping to regenerate a broken and exhausted city.

11 June 1975 The installation of David Sheppard as the sixth Bishop of Liverpool. He was to become one of the best known Bishops in the country, famous for his close working friendship with Roman Catholic Archbishop Derek Worlock. Together they formed an active and powerful ecumenical symbol in the city and beyond.

Opposite The Albert Dock in 1984 shortly after its first phase of renovation. The block to the right of the Cathedral displays bomb damage, which has since been skillfully restored. The Albert Dock, like the Cathedral, is a powerful symbol of the city's regeneration.

At every point in its history, the Liverpool Cathedral community has reached forward with hope and their achievement has become a visible symbol of hope for the wider community. In the dreariest days of the depressed eighties, the slow developments over the road from the Cathedral were helping to regenerate a broken city. The Very Reverend Derrick Walters, fourth Dean of Liverpool, brought unique skills to the city and his 'little Cathedral'.

TODAY AND TOMORROW

"They are places where it is still possible for experiments to be essayed, where independent voices may be allowed, where excellence can be achieved in liturgy, music, art and design, and even, still, in scholarship" Edward Norman

"Flexibility is the key ... Indeed, I believe that our Cathedrals will only survive into the future if they become dynamic centres of experiment." Edward Patey

"Liberty to Grow" Frederick Dwelly

"Vision and labour and sacrifice and generosity indeed. We owe it to them to put the highest value on the legacy we have received, to take seriously the questions we must ask about it; we hold the Cathedrals in trust on their behalf, for now and for the future." Susan Hill

"We must build for posterity," declared Bishop Chavasse in the Town Hall in 1901. I wonder how the good people who embarked on the whole Cathedral project over a hundred years ago would view their city and their great Cathedral in the early years of the twenty-first century?

The gigantic building project on St James's Mount ~ Cathedral, houses, and university buildings ~ are in one sense a twentieth century time line linking the aspirations of Bishop Chavasse through to the urban regeneration schemes of Derrick Walters. The city built its unignorable Cathedral, surely one of the great church buildings of the world, but it was a battered and exhausted city that set the final stones in place. Even the most visionary of the early builders could not have had any idea as to how that building would be used and how it would lead and serve the community who built it. Of course, the statutory daily and weekly services of the Church of England have been celebrated without interruption, despite poverty, war, social unrest, urban decay and a drift away from the Church. From the inspirational years of Dean Dwelly onwards, the special services have been great works of art combining words, music and movement in such a way as to appeal strongly to a vast cross-section of worshippers. Any Cathedral faces the constant danger that the community is too turned in upon itself, intent only upon serving the needs of its resident congregation, but across the decades the Cathedral has striven to serve the changing needs of the city that built it. The founding fathers had no thoughts of a whole season of symphony concerts, professional drama, dance, exhibition, pop concert, lecture, craft displays, hundreds of school parties, conferences and university graduations. Those who balked at the very idea of employing an architect who was a Roman Catholic could never have dreamed of the ecumenical developments of Sheppard and Warlock and the joint, Two Cathedrals Services at Pentecost.

The city in the early years of the twenty-first century emanates a sense of optimism clearly discernible in the range and scale of its new buildings. On the morning of Tuesday June 2003, Bishop James Jones, for the only time in his life, had his mobile phone turned on during the early service in the Lady Chapel. At 8.10am he received a text message to inform him that Liverpool had won the competition for European Capital of Culture 2008. There could have been no place more appropriate for him to receive the good news than in his Cathedral, a Cathedral which had shown itself to be one of the significant cultural centres within a great city.

Annually in the Cathedral, on the Sunday in July nearest in date to the 1924 Consecration Service, there is a simple ceremony which makes the most powerful statement about the Cathedral, past, present and future. During the Choral Eucharist, the youngest chorister walks down from the Chancel to the eastern crossing carrying a small bowl of water and a brush. As the choir sings, he paints the Alpha and Omega Consecration Mark with water that makes the inscription shine for the rest of the service. The Cathedral community remembers the past with gratitude, takes stock of the present and looks forward with dedication to the future. Though the stones may be in place and the fabric complete, the building of a Cathedral, and a city, is a process which never ends.

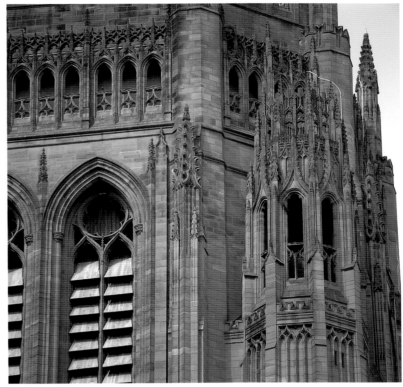

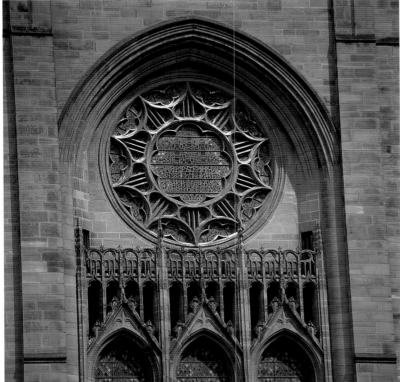

1993 Opposite Dame Elizabeth Frink's *Risen Christ* figure in bronze was unveiled over the west doors of the Cathedral. She had never visited the Cathedral before taking up the commission. In the words of her biographer, Stephen Gardiner, "She had imagined that Sir Giles Scott's twentieth-century Cathedral would be another boring Neo-Gothic building. Wrong ~ she found it marvellous and was captivated by its atmosphere".

Above and left The most cursory look at the Cathedral reveals a wealth of detail. Even in those parts of the building away from close scrutiny, the level of craftsmanship is maintained at the highest level.

Opposite With a building as vast as Liverpool Cathedral, the observer sometimes needs the lens of the skilled photographer to begin to reveal some of the superb details. The exuberance of the stone carver is revealed in many external features, of no structural significance, but everywhere providing fascinating details which can be appreciated only at close quarters.

Above The quality of the detail along the top of the bronze gates on the Rankin Porch.

Opposite The skills of the stone carver and the lead worker combine to produce an arresting feature at the top of a down spout high up on the Chapter House. A feature hardly discernible from the ground.

Top three Grotesque human figures.

Bottom five The Liverpool sculptor, Edward Carter Preston, provided more carved figures for the fabric of the Cathedral than any other artist. These statues from the Rankin Porch depict figures from the parables of Jesus. The one in the bottom right corner is of Mrs Carter Preston. Many of these figures were actually carved in sandstone by carver Reginald Yorke.

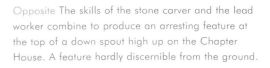

126   Procession through the central space at an ordination service in 2003.

View from the west end of the Cathedral through the soaring piers towards the High Altar. Scott wanted the arch of the bridge to frame the reredos and High Altar. It is not surprising that the word used by most visitors when they see this view is 'Wow!'

128   View from the gallery over the Rankin Porch doors across the central space towards the bridge and the west window.

View from the top of the bridge down into what is technically the nave of the Cathedral.

Studies in light and shade, texture, line, angle and colour around the nave bridge.

132   The staggering view from the Corona Gallery just below the under-tower vaulting. This vantage point is not for the faint-hearted, or anyone suffering from vertigo.

View upwards from the Scott Memorial, the very centre of the Cathedral floor, to the under-tower vaulting and the bell trap. 133

134   A view seen by very few from the little circular gallery just below the roof of the octagonal Chapter House.

Opposite Arches and doorways. Clockwise from the top right: Chapter House, arch and steps up from the ambulatory into the sanctuary, south choir aisle, interior of the west doors.

135

136

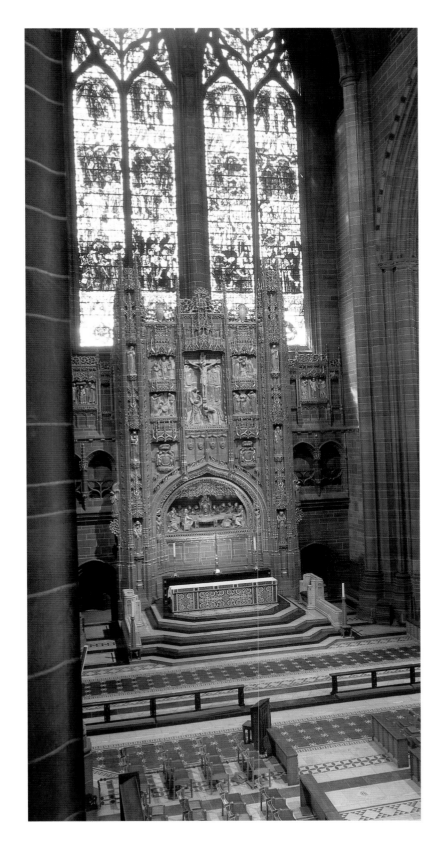

The High Altar against the elaborate sandstone reredos is the focal point of the whole building. The reredos was designed by Giles Scott, but the figure-work was a result of the collaboration between Louis Weingartner and Walter Gilbert. The Lady Chapel reredos focuses upon the Nativity and the beginning of Christ's Ministry. The High Altar reredos draws the eye and the mind to the Last Supper and the Crucifixion. The panels on either side of the reredos depict Nativity on the left and Resurrection on the right.

Lady Chapel from the gallery below the organ at the west end. The chapel rivals many parish churches in size.

Lady Chapel looking towards the organ and the west end. The chapel is more ornate and richly decorated than the main body of the Cathedral.

Details within the Lady Chapel. The reredos was designed jointly by GF Bodley and Giles Scott. The figures of carved painted wood depict incidents from the beginning of Christ's earthly ministry.

Opposite Vaulting in the Lady Chapel.

View across the central space, over the Scott Memorial, to the inner doors of the
Rankin Porch, with elegant Carter Preston figures representing the arts and the sciences.

Opposite Door embellishments revealing the skills of the metal workers.

142

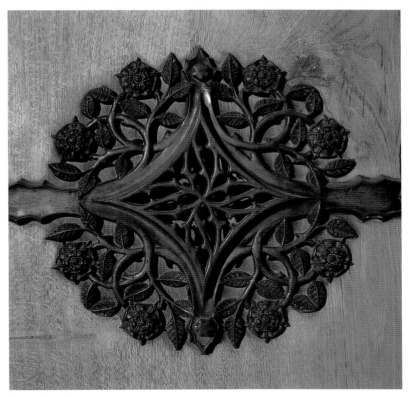

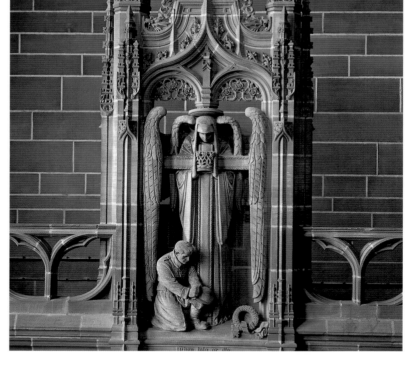

Above Light and shade through one of the Gospel windows, high up on the south side of the Chancel.

Right Full view and a detail from the 55th West Lancashire Division memorial.

Opposite Carved stone angels rarely noticed by the casual visitor.

An orchestra of carved oak angels on the ends of the choir pews.

148   View down into the bell chamber housing the highest and heaviest peal of bells anywhere in the world.

The ringers in position in the ringing chamber.

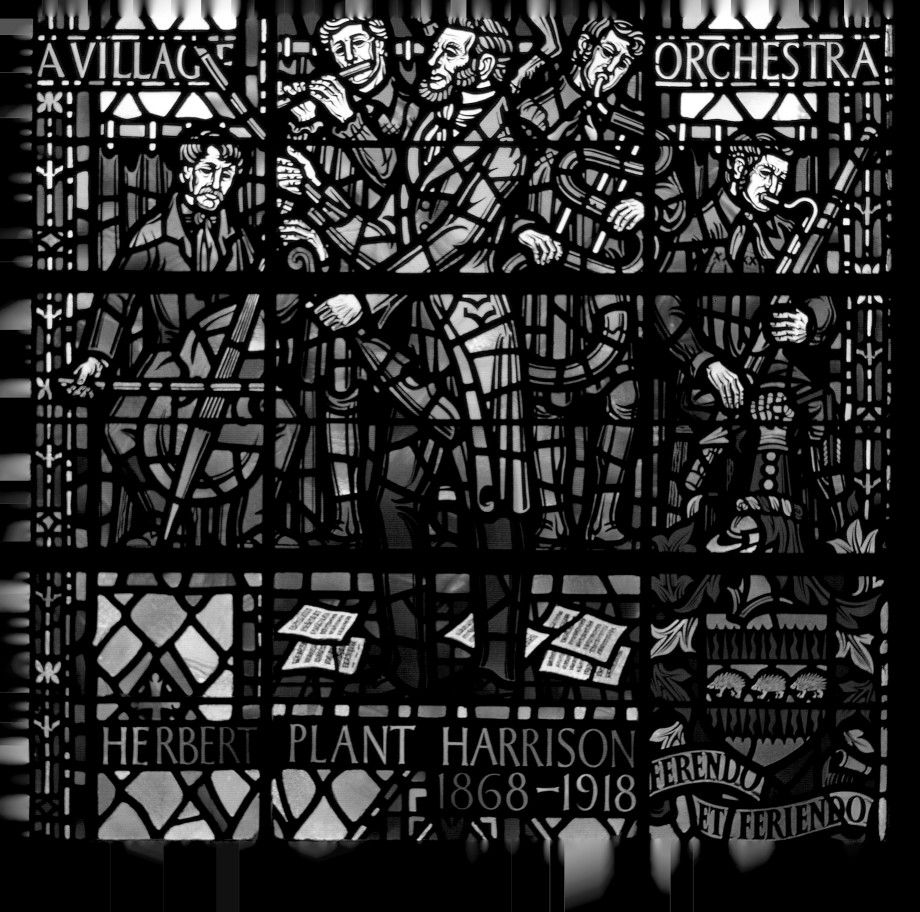

A VILLAGE ORCHESTRA

HERBERT PLANT HARRISON
1868-1918

FERENDO ET FERIENDO

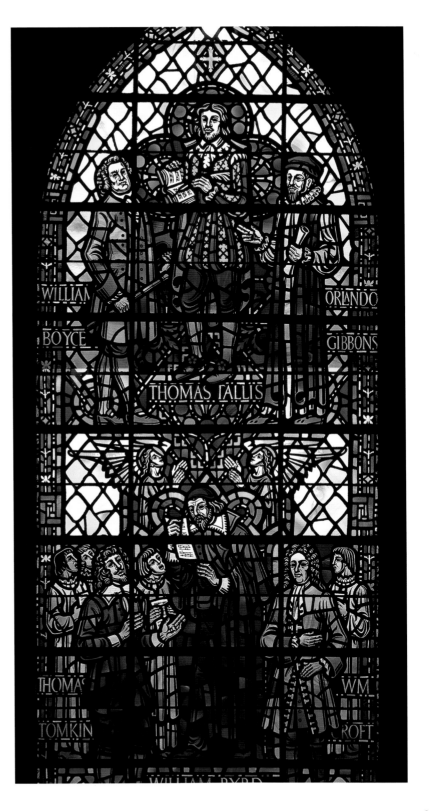

Details from the Musicians' Window on the north side of the nave.

152   The upper portion of the west window. It is the largest window in the Cathedral and covers an area of 1,600 square feet.

St Francis, Mary Magdalene and Martha in the west window.

This page More details from Carl Edwards's west window. To record the window, the photographer was suspended on a rope.

Opposite Sections of two lancets of the Laymen's Window depicting many of the people responsible for the building and its furnishings.

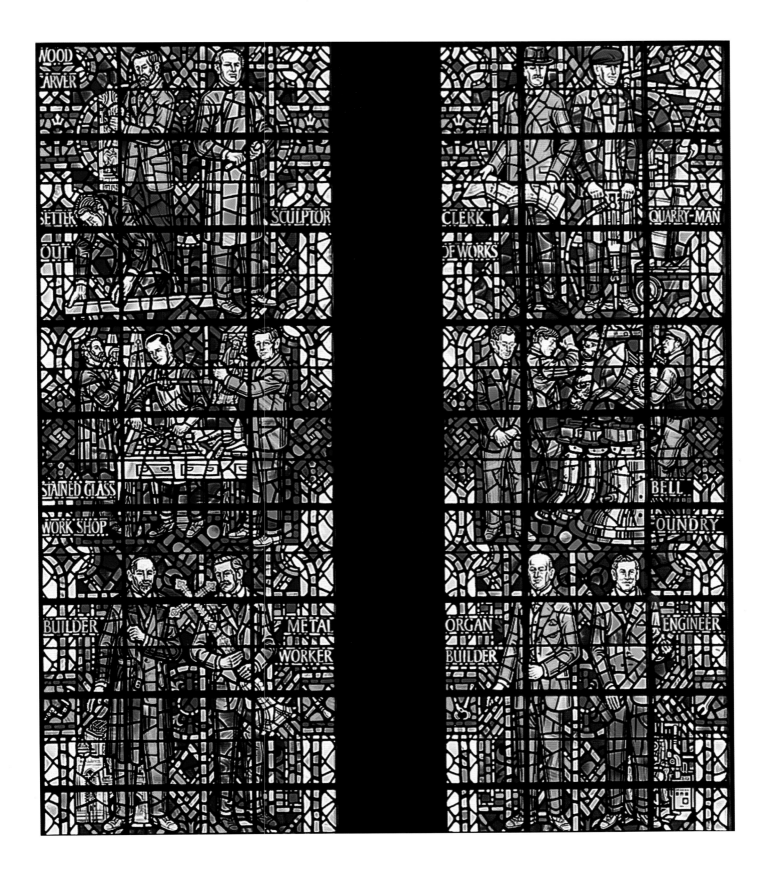

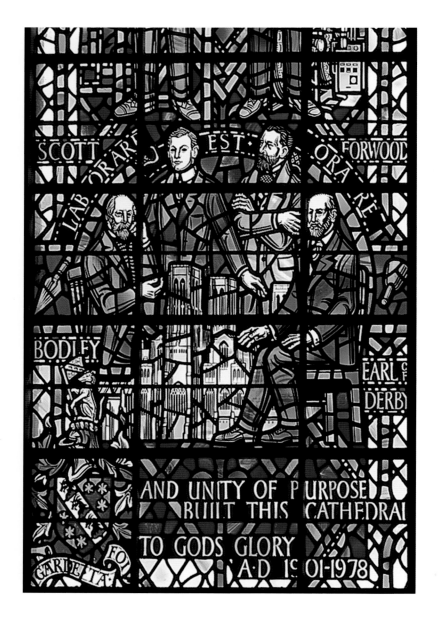

Detail from the Laymen's Window. The figure in the blue jacket is Giles Gilbert Scott.

Detail from the Bishops' Window. Bishop Chavasse is on the right.

Consecration of Liverpool Cathedral in the presence of King George V and Queen Mary in the north west transept window

Not part of a window but a small panel made by Alfred Fisher, a former member of the choir, to commemorate the dedication of the bells.

158   Nativity panel from the New Testament under-tower window – the work of James Hogan.   Opposite The Patron Saint of music from the top of the Musicians' Window.

O Lord God, when thou givest to thy servants to endeavour any great matter, grant us also to know that it is not the beginning, but the continuing of the same, until it be thoroughly finished, which yieldeth the true glory; through him who for the finishing of thy work laid down his life for us, our Redeemer, Jesus Christ. Prayer of Sir Francis Drake